THE
Confidence Project
JOURNAL

52 Journal Prompts to Uncover Personal Strength and Stop Self-Doubt

Kaity Rodriguez, MSW, LCSW

HIGHLANDER
PRESS

Published by: Highlander Press
501 W University Pkwy, Suite B2
Baltimore, MD 21210

Editor: Deborah Kevin
Cover and Layout Design: Pat Creedon Design, Inc.
Author Photo: J. Martin Productions

Hardcover: 978-1-7343764-7-0
Paperback: 978-1-7343764-8-7

EDICATION

TO IVIE

This book is dedicated to the woman you will become.
I wrote part of it sitting with your mom, who encour-
aged me to write to little girls and their unicorns. That
was inspired by you. My hope is that your confidence
will allow you to forever be as bright and shining as you
are right now—at six years old. But should life weigh you
down and make you forget who you are, you have this
journal to help you find your way. ~ Aunt Kaity

TO MY FORMER CLIENTS

You know—the ladies who put in the work.
You fall down and cry and ALWAYS get back up.
You will get where you're going…you always do ;-)
This one is for you. ~ Kaity

TABLE OF CONTENTS

*I*NTRODUCTION

"What's wrong with me?"
That was the resounding question reverberating throughout my mind. I was twenty-seven years old and an anxious wreck. I had just ended a seven-year relationship, was adjusting to a new job, and regularly saw kids who cut themselves on purpose. All of this proved to be a perfect storm of events that sent me into an emotional hurricane and clinical anxiety.

Just two years earlier, I had been standing on the stage of the Miss USA pageant, representing my home state, New Jersey. I spoke to crowds of youth about reaching their dreams, performed on live T.V. in front of millions, and wore a swimsuit on stage without even flinching. I was the picture of confidence…at least on the outside.

My inner world told a much different story. Most people consider the pageant world to be all glitz, glamour, and world peace. It's far from it. I experienced criticism that made my middle school years seem like a cakewalk. People called me names, compared my features to those of animals, and tossed around all forms of racial slurs as they cast their predictions for who would win the title of Miss USA. Even well-meaning family members and friends would give unsolicited advice on how I should look. I can still remember holding back tears at an appearance one day. A person who I considered to be a mother figure at the time casually mentioned to me how I needed to pull my look together to be more like that of a beauty queen. I was crushed.

On top of the external criticism, there were the comparisons I made in my own mind. Before going off to Las Vegas to compete for Miss USA, I had the opportunity to meet my fellow contestants. They were all gorgeous, intelligent, and amazing young women, many of whom were already working as models in the industry. I compared these women to my five feet four inches, non-modeling, acne-prone self, and felt completely inferior.

It's no wonder I fell into a pit of anxiety, culminating in a series of panic attacks and one trip to the E.R. just a few years later.

Fortunately, those panic attacks led me to start therapy, where healing began. I learned that I had never learned to trust myself and my ability to make sound decisions, the perfect breeding ground for anxiety, so I didn't believe I could bounce back from mistakes and failure or rejection. I had not made peace with my flaws. I valued the opinions of others over my opinion of myself. That's why the criticism hurt so badly.

My time in therapy made me so much more self-aware. As a therapist, I can say in full confidence that awareness is the precursor to healing and growth. In fact, I believe in self-awareness so much that I've made it the foundation of *The Confidence Journal*!

If you've picked up this journal, you may be struggling to realize what makes you amazing. You could need a reminder about your own strength. Perhaps you're simply tired of playing small because you're unsure of whether or not you have what it takes to squeeze out of life all of the juicy goodness that it has to offer.

Whatever your reason for picking up this journal, prepare to rediscover yourself. Throughout these fifty-two journal entries, you will chart your goals and dreams and outline your spiritual beliefs. You will travel back in time to revisit some of your most bright and shining moments, as well as some of your darkest challenges. You will take your self-awareness to new heights. Be careful…you might just surprise yourself!

"Why am I always so negative?"

Failure is an essential part of a life well-lived. We strive, and sometimes we hit the mark. Other times, we fail miserably. If we're not aware, these failures become a part of our personal narratives, darkening how we feel and limiting our potential.

"I was rejected from that school; therefore, I'm a reject and will probably never be successful."

"My marriage failed; therefore, I'm bad at relationships and better off alone."

"I lost my temper and yelled at my kids today; so, I must be a bad mother."

As I looked back on my own response to failures in life, I began to ask myself a series of questions: "Why do we hang on to failures and define ourselves by them, rather than the times that we succeed? Why do we focus intently on correcting our flaws, rather than maximizing our strengths? What causes us to forget the five compliments we received at work, but hold on to that one critical comment? Why does the negative seem so much more bitter than the positive sweet?"

Blame it on negativity bias.

The negativity bias is a biological dynamic that is primitive in nature and common among all humans. It goes back to our survival instinct. Our brains are wired to sense impending danger, lack, and general threats to our wellness. Whether it was the saber-tooth tiger lurking in the bushes alluding to certain death during our early days, or the crater-sized forehead pimple inferring rejection and isolation today, our brains are wired to zero in on what's dangerous, defective, or undesirable. At its most basic level, this awareness allows us to react and (hopefully) save ourselves.

While your brain may be wired to magnify what's negative or threatening in nature, fear not! You are not doomed to be subject to your negative thoughts. There is hope! It is possible to reduce the impact of the negativity bias as it pertains to how you feel about yourself. The key is to be intentional.

You must be intentional about seeking out the positive in your life. You must search for it relentlessly as if your very life depends on it. Because in a sense, doesn't it? The life you want is on the other side of all your doubts, fears, and judgments about what is possible. You will need to be intentional about working through your bias because you're challenging your natural wiring and millennia of genetic programming. It's no easy task.

Be intentional about searching for the positive within yourself and all that you have to be confident about. It's easy (natural even) to focus on what's "wrong" with you. But have you searched for what's right?

This is the goal of *The Confidence Project Journal*. We will be taking you on a journey to celebrate what's right, strong, beautiful, and courageous in your life. Failures may have overshadowed it. Critics may indicate otherwise. Life's trials may have caused you to forget it…but greatness still lives inside of you!

WHO ARE YOU?

"We oft know little of who we were, only something of who we are, and nothing of who we may be."

Charlie Fletcher, Silvertongue

The Confidence Project Journal was written to help you examine who you are in a way that will spark self-appreciation. Let's start by examining who you believe you are today. How would you describe yourself to a stranger? *Who exactly are you?* What makes you who you are? Once you have written about who you are, write about how you feel describing yourself. Do you feel positive, proud, ashamed, or uncertain? This entry may take some time to uncover and may not come easily...because it's such a huge question! If you haven't had much time for self-exploration lately, give yourself time and expect a little uncertainty or even tension (that's where the growth happens). There are no "right" or "wrong" answers, only your personal truth.

STRENGTH OVER WEAKNESS

"Don't push your weaknesses.
Play with your strengths."
Jennifer Lopez

"I'm terrible at working out." "My handwriting is atrocious." "I'm a terrible cook." So often, we focus on the deficits and weaknesses that we see in ourselves. As we verbalize these weaknesses time after time, they begin to color the way we see ourselves. We begin to see a canvas full of problems, errors, and deficits.

The truth is that many of our flaws will always be with us, no matter how hard we try to change them. To be human is to be flawed, and guess what? *To be flawed is perfectly okay!*

A better use of energy is to focus on our strengths. We can allow the awareness of our strong points to guide our decisions and set the tone for how we feel about ourselves. We can divert our energy to make our strengths even stronger and shine a light on our areas of giftedness.

In today's journal, list the things that you do well. How did you discover these strengths? What can you do to further develop or enjoy them?

$\mathcal{A}$ SPIRITUAL GROUNDING

"I am fearfully and wonderfully made."
Psalms 139:14

Being confident begins with understanding and knowing who we are. Many of us will spend our entire lives trying to discover who we are and what we believe. We will look at other people, achievements, and past experiences to inform us. The problem is that none of these sources provide us with a fixed assessment. Other people may sing our praises when we're making them happy and then curse us once we stop meeting their needs. Achievement is wonderful, but what happens when we inevitably fail? Past failures are the worst assessors. They fail to account for what we have learned, how we have grown, and what is possible. A self-assessment based on a past that is filled with mistakes and pain will lead us to think that we have little value and significance in the world.

The best assessment of who we are will be found through a higher source. As only the inventor can explain the value and purpose of the invention, only the power that created us can inform us of our value and who we really are. What does your higher power say about you? Write about your spiritual convictions and what they say about your inherent value and potential. Take your time with this entry; it may require some research.

$\mathcal{F}$LAWS AND ALL

*"Be who you are and say what you feel
because those who mind don't matter, and those who
matter don't mind."*

Dr. Seuss

Self-love, something even greater than confidence, comes when we can accept who we are, *as* we are. As I'm sure you know, NONE of us are perfect. We are all a mixed gumbo of emotions, mistakes, flaws, and challenges. Paradoxically, amid all that mess, we are still magical, miraculous, and limitless. We are all conduits of love, talent, joy, and grace. When put to proper use, all that we are and all that we've been through can be utilized for the betterment of this world; but first, we must accept it…in the words of Beyoncé…" flaws and all."

In order to be all that we were created to be *and* truly love ourselves, we must accept ourselves. We must accept the "gumbo," the flaws that we cannot change, along with the gifts. We must decide that even if those flaws never change, we are still worthy of love and capable of greatness. Why? Because all human beings are worthy of love and capable of greatness. With that decision, comes freedom.

Now, here's the kicker (I'm sure you'll love this part). Acceptance doesn't mean we will give up trying to improve whatever the problem may be. It means that until it changes (*if* it changes) we will not criticize, reject, shame or punish ourselves because of it.

What do you accept about yourself? With what will you decide to make peace, even if you don't like it? What will you no longer do as a form of self-rejection?

I will work to accept	I will no longer do the following as a form of self-rejection
My body	Buy or hold onto clothing that is too small, hoping it will motivate me to change.

THE BEST DAY EVER

"You can become blind by seeing each day as a similar one. Each day is a different one, each day brings a miracle of its own. It's just a matter of paying attention."

Paulo Coelho

There are moments in our lives through which we are forever changed. Maybe it's a wedding day, long-awaited graduation, or the birth of a child. These moments alter our worldview and challenge us to grow. They show us the superpowers we possess.

If placed under a microscope, these moments will show us some of the best we have.

Reflect on your best day. Detail what happened and how it made you feel. How did you show up on that day? Were you strong, joyful, at peace? On your not-so-good days, remember how you showed up on that day. The same strength, joy, peace, etc. still lay within you. They will emerge again…if you allow them.

SURFACE LEVEL

"Beauty is when you can appreciate yourself."

Zoe Kravitz

Let's face it. While internal beauty is the ultimate goal, external beauty ain't half bad either. While it may only be surface level that doesn't mean it doesn't matter. Most women want to feel beautiful and sexy in their own skin. AND all women have that capacity. We are made in the image and likeness of God, so we all have beautiful external features.

So often as women, we think it's arrogant or conceited to verbalize or even acknowledge our own beauty. This is a myth. Acknowledging your own beauty is healthy and promotes confidence.

It's also important to know what forms of beauty are important to you–and only you–not what the media, pop culture or your ex told you is physically attractive. What's appealing to you, as a woman, of your age, ethnicity, and world view? As women, we have to empower ourselves to create our own definitions–even of physical beauty.

Today's journal requires less soul searching, but it may require some mirror work. What are your favorite physical features, and how can you fully appreciate them? If you're unsure, go to the mirror and search. Maybe it's the tone of your skin, so you will decide to wear a bit of bronzer to add a bit of sparkle. Maybe it's your smile, so you will smile more often or even wear red lipstick. Perhaps you love your eyes because they light up when your smile, so you will trade your glasses for contacts. Or maybe you simply love your long legs and will buy a few short skirts! Don't skip this entry, and don't be afraid to stand out. Find at least one feature and journal about how you can fully appreciate this feature. Don't be afraid to toot your own horn. Let's talk about the beauty that runs on the surface.

DIGGING DEEPER

"Though we travel the world over to find the beautiful, we must carry it with us or we find it not."

Ralph Waldo Emerson

Now that you've taken a moment to acknowledge our physical beauty, let's go a bit deeper. While physical beauty is wonderful, it is also fleeting. Skin wrinkles, hair turns grey, and bones creak. We short-change ourselves when we build the foundation of our self-worth upon shifting sands. What matters more is that we know the beautiful nature of our hearts, which only grow with time…if we allow it.

In today's journal, take some time to explore your inner beauty. What kind of person do you strive to be daily? What values do you uphold? What aspects of your personality are admirable? Don't skip this entry. If you're struggling, ask someone who loves you to help you with this entry.

THE TRAIL HAS BEEN BLAZED

"I am a man, nothing human can be alien to me."

Terence

At the most basic level, we are simply humans—imperfect and prone to make mistakes. We will inevitably experience anger, fear, doubt, and insecurity. We will fail and fall short…because we are human.

However, there is another side of our humanity.

While we are "only human," with that comes extraordinary capability. When we're uncertain of our own capabilities, we need not look far to find answers. The world around us will tell us what we need to know. The same basic traits that made the world's most extraordinary people can be found within all of us.

Just think about that. The same characteristics that made Maya Angelou, Oprah Winfrey, Albert Einstein, and Mother Teresa have made you too! You have the same basic cell structure and capacity to love or hate. No matter how great these trailblazers were, they were human—just like you. Nothing about them can be completely alien to you.

In today's journal, write about your role models. What parts of them can you see in yourself? They've already blazed the trail for you, so how are you following in their footsteps? How do you draw from their strengths and carry them with you daily?

THE POWER IN THE PLAN

"Write the vision down and make it plain upon tables so that he may run who reads it."

Habakkuk 2:2

Imagine that a friend invited you to come to visit her in her new home a few towns over. Excited about the visit and ready to reconnect with your bestie whom you haven't seen in months, you quickly jump in your car and head in her direction. However, along the way to the town, you encounter a problem. You realize that you have no idea where you're going. She never gave you her new address. Without thinking, you set off in the direction of her old home, as you have so many times in the past.

Once you realize your error, you pull over to try calling but get no answer. You remember her mentioning a neighborhood and drive in that direction, but the further you get, the more frustrating and ridiculous the trip becomes. You know you can't drive all over the city knocking on every door. You're frustrated that she's not answering and scolding yourself for forgetting to ask for the address, so you turn to head home. Finally, she calls and gives you an address. It took you twice the time it would normally have taken because you had no direction.

The same is true in our lives. We need direction. Few great achievements just happen. Rather, they are the result of years of planning and intentional decisions. To be intentional, we start by determining what we want as the end result (the address). This gives us direction and reduces the frustration of driving all over aimlessly. It increases our confidence in our ability to experience success.

What are your goals, dreams, and aspirations? Dig deep as you explore the personal, as well as the professional. List a few for each category as well as a timeline to keep you accountable. How can you go about achieving these goals?

Goal: Save $10,000	By When? January 1
Action 1	Consult with financial advisor
Action 2	Open savings account
Action 3	Set up direct deposit
Goal:	By When?
Action 1	
Action 2	
Action 3	
Goal:	By When?
Action 1	
Action 2	
Action 3	
Goal:	By When?
Action 1	
Action 2	
Action 3	
Goal:	By When?
Action 1	
Action 2	
Action 3	

# HER BIGGEST WIN

"What lies behind us and what lies before us
are tiny matters compared to what lies within us."

Ralph Waldo Emerson

As human beings, we all have wells of untapped potential lying dormant inside, waiting to be awoken. We've landed on the moon and created bionic limbs. We can even video with loved ones across the globe…for free! As a species, we have accomplished some pretty amazing things.

Every once in a while—maybe just a few times in life—we surprise ourselves and do something that is nothing short of utterly amazing. It is a stunning demonstration of the untapped potential we possess and has the capacity to change us deeply. These moments should be documented, hung on a wall, and referenced every time life presents us with challenges that question our fortitude.

Reflect on your greatest win. What did that accomplishment require of you? What life lessons did you gain throughout the process?

THE WINNER'S CIRCLE

"A great accomplishment shouldn't be the end of the road, just the starting point for the next leap forward."
Harvey Mackay

Confidence is the result of continuous effort, matched with successful outcomes over a given period. Take riding a bike, for example. When our training wheels are first removed, we are nervous and unconfident in our ability to remain upright. We fall down and skin our knees, but hopefully, keep trying. Eventually, we gain an understanding of how to balance ourselves. Soon, we become experts, riding for as long and as far as we desire—or as far as our parents will allow. We are no longer uncertain, but confident because we REMEMBER the success. Even with mastering the skill of riding, if we do not remember our success, we will be nervous and uncertain with each new mount.

Sometimes we feel uncertain about our ability to succeed in life—about our ability to accomplish our goals and become who we have set out to be. We fail to REMEMBER our past accomplishments and successes. Doing so would enable us to re-acknowledge the often difficult process of achievement, as well as our own ability to prevail.

You've already recorded your greatest accomplishment, but I'm sure there's more. In today's journal entry, look back on your past successes and accomplishments. Remember those great and small. Reflect on the process and how those experiences can strengthen your journey and increase your confidence today. What did it take for you to stand in the winner's circle?

$\mathcal{A}$ BRIGHT AND SHINING MOMENT

"A photo is worth a thousand words."

Unknown

At times, the dark moments we encounter cast gloomy shadows that can darken the entire tapestry of life. The bright and joyous moments seem to be too far lost in the past to ever recover. If we're not mindful, the discouragement and pain from the battles of life make us forget our own vibrancy. Heartache can make us forget the passion of falling in love. Failure causes us to forget the pride of our past success. The grief of loss makes us question what we have to be grateful for in the first place.

During these moments, we need to be reminded of our own power. If pride, joy, and strength were once yours, they never leave your possession. They may lay covered and dormant. They may evolve and transform, but they are yours for the keeping. You just have to access them.

In this journal, attach a photo of yourself that captured you in one of your brightest moments. It may have been a precious moment shared between you and a loved one. Perhaps it was the celebration of a major accomplishment. Or maybe it's a simple photo of you, still and peaceful. What draws you to this image of yourself? What does it tell you about yourself? What aspects of that person can you carry with you today?

If you can't access one of these photos, take one today. Today is the oldest and wisest you've ever been and the youngest you will ever be again. Why not capture it?

SAY HELLO TO YOUR FUTURE

"Most people overestimate what they can do in one year and underestimate what they can do in ten years."
Bill Gates

Have you ever stopped to imagine the woman you will be twenty years from now? Not just one or two things that you would like to do, but a detailed concept of the person that you will become. Life can cause us to become so wrapped up in where we are right now, along with our flaws, shortcomings, and unfinished business, that our self-concepts become weighed down and stagnant. We forget about what's possible.

Visiting ourselves in the future can help. Not taking a trip in a time machine, but taking time to consider who, how, and where we will be as we grow older. Taking time to imagine our future selves, fully actualized, wise, and fulfilled, can help inform our decisions in the present. It can also awaken us to the understanding that most issues in this life are temporary. The problems and weaknesses that we have today do not have to be problems and weaknesses a few years from now. If they are, they might not even matter much!

Imagining our future selves can be exciting and motivating as we realize that we have the power to determine who we want to be. Of course, life will cause us to take some twists and turns. We might not land exactly where we plan, but we do not have to be victims of our circumstances, blowing whichever way life takes us.

The woman you desire to become is already inside of you; she's just waiting to be released. In today's journal, introduce the woman you will be twenty years from now. What is she like? Where does she live? What does she do for work and play? How does she feel and live? Go deep and give a detailed description. Then, let that woman lead your decisions today. What shifts do you need to make in your present to honor that woman in your future?

TRUE LOVE HAS NO LIMITS

"Spread love everywhere you go.
Let no one ever come to you without leaving happier."
Mother Teresa

Unconditional love (love without expectation or stipulation), is the greatest power in the universe. It is the power that causes a new mother to weep with delight. It opens the wounded children of ill-equipped parents to the power of forgiveness. It even prompts puppy parents to smile past chewed shoes and destroyed furniture. When we exhibit this form of love, we are perhaps the closest to being one with God. It is a beautiful state to abide in and brings out the best we have to offer.

We all have the capacity for unconditional love. Acknowledging its presence in our lives awakens us to our own strength and godliness.

Journal about your experience with unconditional love. How have you, and how can you continue to express this form of love?

*O*H! HAPPY DAY

"Being happy never goes out of style."

Lily Pulitzer

To be happy is to radiate positivity. We dance, sing, and maybe even smile at strangers. The dopamine released in our brains energizes us, and we're motivated to accomplish more and perform better. We're better able to look on the bright side and acknowledge all that is well in life. Happy is a beautiful way to be.

Although we cannot always operate in a state of happiness, it's important to remember that we all have the capacity to be happy. Yes, despite how life has beaten you up and knocked you down, you still have the ability to experience joy…even if it's been a long, long time. The capacity lies not within your circumstances, but between your ears.

What are you like when you're happy? How do those closest to you know that you're happy? Write about how you express emotion. If it's been a while since you've been happy, it might be time to commit to intentional happiness. What do you need to change in your life to experience happiness and gratitude? What simple things make you happy? How can you be intentional about making space for those things in your life?

AM

"Identity is the role you chose to play in the story of the Universe."

Maria V. Shall

Ever hear a loving mother tell her child, "You can be anything you want to be?" It's beautiful and encouraging and filled with hope. But is it true? Often times as we grow older, we lose childlike belief in ourselves and the idea of becoming "anything we want to be." Failures, derailment, and heartache cause us to forget our own powers. Nevertheless, mama wasn't lying.

We can, in fact, be anything we want to be; however, we must first *decide* to do so. Being confident, joyful, on time, or even the president of the United States rarely (if ever) happens by accident. It requires intentional effort. The first step in being intentional is by deciding to do so. We must make a declaration about who we are and who we intend to be. The phrase "I am" is a powerful one. Whatever follows, it will tell us and the rest of the world what to expect of us. It gives us direction for the day and sets our behaviors in motion. Choose wisely.

So who are you? How are you? What are you? In today's journal, write a list of "I am" statements.

I am: A woman with the power to give life
I am:
I am:
I am:
I am:
I am:
I am:
I am:
I am:
I am:
I am:
I am:
I am:
I am:
I am:
I am:
I am:
I am:
I am:
I am:

OVERCOMING DOUBT

*"Our doubts are traitors and make us lose the good
we oft might win by fearing to attempt."*
William Shakespeare

The fear response is simply our body's built-in protection mechanism. When lions and tigers and bears are nearby, this innate response will serve us and keep us safe from physical danger. However, most often, the fear that we experience today has nothing to do with physical danger. The silent, untouchable predators that most of us currently avoid are rejection, embarrassment, and failure.

Fear is not to be ignored, it serves a purpose and informs us of what our approach to danger should be. It can keep us safe from predators and physical threats, as well as the less tangible dangers like shame and disappointment. However, fear will never keep us happy or fulfilled. In fact, fear can tell outright lies!

Fear uses doubt to make us believe that we are incapable and unworthy. If we can doubt ourselves enough, we won't have to face the threats of failure or embarrassment; nor will we experience the rewards of success and achievement, because we will never even try. In these cases, we need to be fully aware of our fear but not take direction from it. In the words of psychologist and author, Susan Jeffers, we "feel the fear and do it anyway."

Can you catch fear in a lie? Write about a time that you initially doubted yourself, worked through your fear and emerged successfully. You may also choose to write about how might your life be different if you faced your fears?

THE CHILD WITHIN

"See the world as if for the first time; see it through the eyes of a child, and you will suddenly find that you are free."

Deepak Chopra

If you've ever watched a happy child at play, then you probably understand that they a far more uninhibited than older folks. They shriek with delight and dash around like little bolts of lightning, too fast to catch. They say what's on their minds and dream the biggest dreams. They possess a naïve innocence that safeguards their minds from the dangers of the world.

However, something shifts right around ten years of age. As we become more aware of the world around us, we begin to turn inward. We start to question how we compare with everything and everyone else. We become concerned about how other people view us and wonder whether or not we have the capacity to fulfill our dreams. Welcome to adulthood.

Although we cannot return to our childhoods, we can take inspiration from it. We can remember ourselves as uninhibited, carefree, hopeful, and trusting. This is the core of who we are before the world tries to change us.

In today's journal, reflect on yourself as a child. How were you before fear, doubt, and insecurity ever came to visit? How can you take inspiration from that child and apply it to your life now? What beliefs and behaviors do you need to release? What mindset and activities do you need to get back to? If your childhood was less carefree than most, reflect on the times that were pleasant and hold on to them for this entry.

THE CONFIDENCE CODE

"For the things we have to learn before we can do them, we learn by doing them."

Aristotle

Self-confidence is most often developed in the trenches of conquering a new challenge. For example, a normally confident woman that is also a new mother may initially feel unconfident in her ability to parent her baby. At first, she may struggle, cry, and question whether or not she has what it takes. However, after successfully mothering her baby and realizing that she can, in fact, keep a little human alive and well, she will feel more confident in her ability to mother. She may even eventually decide to go for baby number two, realizing that she is more than able to handle the challenge of motherhood, albeit difficult and, at times, painstaking. As with this new mother, it is perfectly normal for our self-confidence to be challenged; in fact, it is healthy for the human condition.

Because we are typically not born absolutely certain of ourselves and our ability to perform a given task, we must step out on faith and believe that we will rise to the challenge over time. Many supports can help us to make that leap of faith. Confidence hacks like the power stance, hugging yourself, or wearing your favorite outfit can help you to feel more capable of taking on a challenge.

What are the hacks to your confidence code? It may be that perfect red lipstick that makes you feel like a rock star. Perhaps a quick call to your best friend helps you remember how awesome you are. In today's journal, record the tools, activities, and supports that help you feel more prepared to take on a challenge.

SECURE YOUR VALUABLES

"Our bodies are our gardens to which our wills are gardeners."

William Shakespeare

We take care of that which is valued. Whether it is our children, our romantic relationships, or even our cars, we will find the time to attend to the needs of the things we care about.

If you own a car and rely on it to take you everywhere, you make sure it is properly fueled and change the oil every few months. You make sure it gets the maintenance it needs. If you really enjoy your car, you may even take it for a wash and detail every few weeks! If you know that your livelihood and safety is dependent upon that car, the thought of driving the car without oil or with faulty breaks is not an option.

As women, we are no different. When we value ourselves, we care for ourselves. So how do you secure some of your most precious valuables: your physical, emotional, and spiritual wellbeing? Do you maintain your doctor appointments? Are you setting boundaries in your relationships? Do you budget for your future? Self-care goes far beyond spa trips and manicures. Explore how you create space for yourself to be the best version of yourself on all fronts.

If you do not make time for self-care, write a detailed plan of how you plan to begin doing so. Include what you will be doing, the frequency at which you will be doing it, and how you will acquire resources like time and money to allow for your plan.

CAN

*"Alone, we can do so little; together,
we can do so much."*

Helen Keller

No one can do it all. Even the most gifted person is limited in her abilities and flawed in some ways (thank God). Imagine if everyone was perfect and able to "do it all" alone. Life might be quite boring, and there would be no need for community or relationships. Ever seen Stepford Wives?

Many of the great leaders and innovators of this world will tell you that what they lack in skills or knowledge, they make up for through the individuals around them. They utilize the power of the group that dates back to our primitive days. The idea is that humans function best in groups because we can glean off of one another's abilities, rather than just our own.

While we can't all do everything, we can all do something. Whether it be the simple ability to talk and calm an anxious mind or the ability to navigate the wilderness and live off the land, we all have contributions to make.

Rather than considering what you can't do, ask what CAN you do. How do you contribute? Can you make a meal for your family? Do you balance a budget, beautify your surroundings, or make people feel great about themselves?

In today's journal, write about all of the things you CAN do, great and small. Complete the phrase: I CAN ____.

I can: do anything I decide to do.
I can:
I can:
I can:
I can:
I can:
I can:
I can:
I can:
I can:
I can:
I can:
I can:
I can:
I can:
I can:
I can:
I can:
I can:
I can:
I can:
I can:
I can:
I can:
I can:

WHAT DO YOU BELIEVE ABOUT YOURSELF?

"You become what you believe,
not what you think or what you want."

Oprah Winfrey

The world will tell you many things about yourself. Rich. Poor. Successful. Shameful. Fat. Skinny. It will tell you what boxes you fit into, what standards you meet, and what to believe about yourself and your potential. This works wonderfully for our self-concepts when the world gives us positive reviews. But what happens when we don't measure up to the expectations placed upon us? What happens when the world tells us that we are less than desirable? If we don't know who we truly are and what we're capable of, we can fall into a pit of despair and self-loathing, believing that we are no more than the world's gloomy assessment of our present state.

Before the world tells you who you are, make the determination for yourself. Based on what you know about yourself and what you've already experienced in life, determine the positive characteristics that you will use to describe yourself. Survived an illness or traumatic experience? Then you're a fighter. Do people often come to you for advice? Then you're likely very wise. You can even take the qualities that some consider to be negative and flip them around to reflect the positive. "Stubborn" individuals are usually very determined. "Indecisive" people are often very careful. "Crazy" can easily be confused with passion!

In today's journal, make a list of the positive characteristics that describe you. You can also include a list of the words that you will no longer choose to believe about yourself. When you begin to question who you are and what you're capable of, refer to this entry.

This is what I believe about who I am:

I am a fighter

This is what I can work to no longer believe about who I am:

My illness makes me weak.

UNCHARTERED WATERS

*"Do not be too timid and squeamish about
your actions. All life is an experiment."*

Ralph Waldo Emerson

In order to grow and evolve, we must continuously stretch ourselves into new territories and unchartered waters. Trying new endeavors challenges us to stretch ourselves beyond our comfort zones. As we continually become familiar with the unfamiliar, we develop a track record that says, "Hey, I can handle this." Over time, we become more confident, knowing that we can handle discomfort and the unfamiliar.

There is one caveat to this concept of trying new things: we must commit to the challenge. Too often, we give up when the challenge becomes difficult. We sabotage ourselves by saying "It wasn't meant to be" and stop trying to reach the goal. When this happens, we then face two problems: the pain of not reaching the goal AND the self-judgment of not finishing what we start. This is not to say we should never pivot and have to complete everything that we start, even if it no longer serves us. However, know the difference between quitting because you're no longer interested in the goal and quitting because it's hard to reach the goal.

Confidence comes from not only sticking with the task of a new challenge but also from the tremendous growth we experience in the process. In the end, we experience observable growth, and we begin to view ourselves as more dedicated individuals who do not run from challenges.

Journal about the last time that you stepped into unchartered waters, tried something new and eventually saw an improvement in your performance. How did it feel to witness your transformation? What did you learn about yourself as a result? If you're struggling to remember the last time you tried a new endeavor, create an action plan on what your next endeavor will be.

RANDOM ACTS OF KINDNESS

"Try to be a rainbow in someone's cloud."

Maya Angelou

Man was not created to function independently. During our primitive days, our lives literally depended on the safety and unity of the group to fight, hunt, and gather. Advancements in technology and industry may change how we live, but they do not change the fact that human beings function better in groups, caring for one another and providing much-needed companionship. Science backs this up. Studies show that the more isolated a person is, the more prone they will be to depression. If you lived alone through COVID-19, you know that social isolation is no joke. We need one another to survive!

Random acts of kindness like making dinner for a new mom or shoveling your neighbor's sidewalk may seem of no consequence to you, but the recipients of these acts may feel otherwise. Combined, these small acts make a huge impact. They create unity and a sense of comradery. Taking the time to be a rainbow in someone's cloud shows that you are a compassionate and active community member to planet earth. It's kind of a big deal!

Reflect on the moments that you've shown kindness to others. What kind of sacrifice did they require from you? What do these acts show about you and how did they make you feel?

WRESTLING WITH FORGIVENESS

"To err is human, to forgive divine."
Alexander Pope

To forgive someone who has hurt us is one of the most difficult things that life will ask. It will likely cause sleepless nights of soul searching and long days of gut-wrenching rage. Nevertheless, it is necessary… not for our aggressors, but for our own peace of mind and wellbeing.

When we successfully reach a point of forgiveness, we compassionately acknowledge the humanity in others and our common brokenness as inhabitants of this planet. We force anger to release its powerful grip and stare vulnerability in the face. We agree to release the past and look hopefully towards the future. To forgive requires emotional fortitude. Forgiveness is hard work.

Write about a time that you forgave someone. How did you do it? What did that forgiveness do for you? What does that act of forgiveness say about you? How does it feel to reflect back on your own strength? If you've never forgiven anyone, consider who you may need to forgive and how you can go about doing so.

*O*VERCOMING ADVERSITY

*"I am not afraid of storms for I am learning
how to sail my ship."*

Louisa May Alcott

Wouldn't "the easy life" be nice? No adversity. Everything just your way, when you want it, and how you want it. No heartbreak to endure, setbacks to overcome, or pain to suffer. That would be awesome, right?

Or would it?

Although adversity is hell to go through, on the other side of it lies strength, gratitude, and wisdom. We learn about ourselves and life, not in the easy times, but the challenging. Like a patient healed and restored to health, as we fight through adversity we can also develop a deeper appreciation for all that is well.

Whether it be an illness, growing up without privilege, the loss of a relationship, or difficulties at work, it takes strength to weather adversity. Unfortunately, some don't make it out of the storm. Write about a time that you overcame adversity. What have you learned about yourself and life through that experience?

CHANGE THE LENS

"You have the ability to adjust the lens through which you view the world."

Jeffrey Duarte

Ever notice that we can be our own worst critics? Perfectionism, self-doubt, and insecurity blind us to the truth and cast a grey haze over all that we do. Even our victories and strengths are downplayed as we analyze how we could have done better. Sometimes, we just can't see our own strength…at least not with our own eyes.

But what if we used a different set of eyes? What if we looked at ourselves through the eyes of a cherished loved one: perhaps a child, a loving spouse, or a long-time friend. These individuals see our worst and still love us. In their eyes, the good shines brighter than the bad.

In today's journal, change the lens through which you are looking at yourself. Consider how a cherished loved one or friend might describe you. Write a description of you from that person's perspective.

HE PURPOSE DRIVEN LIFE

"Only those who have learned the power of sincere and selfless contribution experience life's deepest joy: true fulfillment."

Tony Robbins

The gift of purpose is something that we've all been given, yet often struggle to receive. In thinking about purpose, many of us become stressed, uncertain, and even depressed believing that there is one central purpose that needs to be discovered early on…otherwise, life is meaningless.

The idea of one singular and monumental purpose is misleading. To have purpose simply refers to contributing to the world in a meaningful way. For some, that purpose may be a lifetime calling, discovered during childhood. However, some of us will discover our purposes while traveling a maze of connected experiences throughout adulthood. Our purpose may also evolve as we go through life. As children become adults, parents will transform in their purpose, no longer tasked with raising little people into responsible adults. Their purposes will be redefined.

Our purpose can even vary day-to-day. When we lend a helping hand, donate to a cause, impart knowledge, or bestow compassion, we are making meaningful contributions to the world. It is possible to set an intention daily about how we will purposely contribute to the day before us. Whether it be visiting an elderly relative, helping a new mother, or holding the door for strangers, we can purposefully contribute to the world daily.

If you're searching for a purpose that is akin to finding the cure to world hunger, you may find yourself frustrated and lost. In today's journal, acknowledge the contributions you make to the world. Doing so will not only help you feel more confident in the value you bring to the world, but over time it may also inform you of a larger purpose for your life.

$\mathcal{P}$ASSION

"I was blessed with talent, but I worked as if I had none."

Kobe Bryant

To be naturally talented is a blessing. Talent opens doors and sparks interest. It gives its master a special edge, and if honed correctly, it can pave the way to great success. Talent is wonderful; however, it can not stand without passion.

It was not talent, but passion is what made Thomas Edison persist through thousands of attempts to create the light bulb. Passion pushed a fifteen-year-old Malala Yousafsai to press forward in her quest to advocate for girl's education rights after an assassination attempt nearly took her life. Passion consumed Michael Jackson to the point that music would often kept him up at night, until he recorded the lyrics and melodies just as he heard them in his head.

Harnessed passion is a beauty to behold. It allows witnesses to catch a glimpse inside the soul, the deepest desires, yearnings, and heartaches of its carrier. If you've ever gotten chills or felt goosebumps while listening to a speech or watching a performance, passion was likely present in the room. Whether it was Mother Teresa passionate about service or Martin Luther King Junior, passionate about equality, passion changes the world.

What are you passionate about? What issues keep you up at night? What activities energize you and spark vibrancy in your life? In today's journal, explore your passions. Whether they have been with you since birth or are just beginning to surface, write about the passions you possess. How do they make you feel when you're able to properly harness them? How can you further nourish these gifts?

NATURALLY GIFTED

"A winner is someone who recognizes his God-given talents, works his tail off to develop them into skills, and uses these skills to accomplish his goals."

Larry Bird

Little Michael seemed to be born an entertainer. When he joined his brothers' band as their youngest member, he immediately stood out as a leader. As he grew older, Michael would compose music in his mind. It pained him when he couldn't transfer his music into reality, the way it presented in his head. It's no surprise that he became the greatest entertainer of all time. Although he worked incredibly hard to take his gift worldwide, there's no doubt that music and entertainment came naturally to Michael Jackson. It was his gift.

Like M.J., we all come into the earth with natural gifts and callings. Although they may be perfected over time, these are not skills that need to be cultivated before they can emerge as strengths. They need not be learned in a classroom or perfected before they begin to make an impact in the world. They are the inborn abilities that come rather easily to us.

Whether it be organization or empathy, science, or art, when properly cultivated, our natural abilities can make a major impact in the world. However, before we can utilize them to change the world, we must first acknowledge these gifts.

What are your natural, God-given talents and abilities? To take this journal a step further, consider how you can maximize these gifts to further impact the world.

THE BODY POSITIVE

"Stop trying to fix your body. It was never broken."

Eve Ensler

Have you ever taken a moment to consider the miracle that is your body? Trillions of cells, systematically creating tissues, creating organs that allow you to live, move, and function…a miracle indeed!

Sometimes we forget all that our bodies do for us. In an effort to nip, tuck, and perfect, we unwittingly devalue the powerful vessel through which we experience life. The same nose that we think is too wide or too long allows us to take in the aromas of freshly baked cookies and calming lavender flowers. Those hips that we curse and squeeze into skinny jeans can also balance babies and bounce them to solace. You know that extra melanin in our skin that some might say makes us too dark? Well, it also protects us from the powerful rays of the sun. Yes, our bodies are wonderful creations.

In today's journal, take some time to reflect on all that your body does for you. How does it serve you, and what has it done that you are grateful for? Even if your body has changed or can no longer do what it did at one point, focus your attention on areas of appreciation.

$\mathcal{E}$XPERIENCE: TEACHER OF ALL

"Know from whence you came. If you know whence you came, there are absolutely no limitations to where you can go."

James Baldwin

Our experiences shape us into who we are. They create our worldview, teach us lessons, and jump-start growth. Our positive experiences give us hope. They show us what's possible and provide us with inspiration and motivation. Although we may wish them away, even our negative and painful experiences can make us better. When we allow for it, they make us stronger and more dynamic as we heal, overcome, and push forward.

Write about some of the experiences that have shaped you into who you are. How have they enabled you to grow into a better person?

A LOVING REMINDER

*"To love a person is to see all of their magic
and remind them of it when they have forgotten."*

Unknown

There is not a person walking the earth who hasn't been tested by life. The challenges we experience as constituents of the imperfect human race can bring even the strongest woman to her knees, making her question her sense of self, her abilities, and overall worth. During these times, it helps to be reminded of who we are by the people who love us the most.

Invite someone who loves you dearly to share this entry with you. It may be a partner, a child, a parent, or even a long-time friend. Ask them to write about how you show up in their lives and what's makes you special to them. Then read their entry and reflect upon it to complete this entry.

$\mathcal{G}$RATITUDE IS THE ATTITUDE

"'Enough' is a feast."
Buddhist Proverb

Ever heard the expression "Don't throw the baby out with the bathwater?" It's a southern idiom that reminds us not to discard that which is valuable while attempting to eliminate that which is undesirable. For many of us, we do just that. We find a flaw, some imperfection or shortcoming, that simply reveals our human nature and inability to be "just right." Rather than regarding it as one small patch in the fabric of our beings, we account for it as the entire tapestry. In an unattainable quest for perfection, we discount all that is admirable about ourselves. We throw out the proverbial baby (our own self-worth and self-acceptance), along with the bathwater (our imperfections).

But what would happen if we shifted our attention away from the flaws to celebrate ourselves? What would it be like to tap into gratitude to appreciate the aspects of ourselves that we often take for granted? Don't wait until you no longer have hair to appreciate the hard-to-tame tresses that you currently possess. Celebrate the fact that you're creative, or passionate, or thoughtful. Have gratitude that you were naturally born a hard worker and can get the job done.

What aspects of yourself are you grateful for? Why are you grateful for these attributes? How can you celebrate and fully appreciate them? If you're unsure of where to start, consider what it might be like to lose some aspect of yourself. Whether it be a body part, natural skill, or personality trait, if you would miss it, then practice gratitude for it.

I am grateful for my: ability to sing.

Because: allows me to express myself and bring joy to others.

I will celebrate and appreciate this by: singing in some form everyday.

I am grateful for my:

Because:

I will celebrate and appreciate this by:

I am grateful for my:

Because:

I will celebrate and appreciate this by:

I am grateful for my:

Because:

I will celebrate and appreciate this by:

I am grateful for my:

Because:

I will celebrate and appreciate this by:

I am grateful for my:

Because:

I will celebrate and appreciate this by:

I am grateful for my:

Because:

I will celebrate and appreciate this by:

I am grateful for my:

Because:

I will celebrate and appreciate this by:

I am grateful for my:

Because:

I will celebrate and appreciate this by:

I am grateful for my:

Because:

I will celebrate and appreciate this by:

THE PRACTICE OF GRATITUDE

*"It is not happy people who are thankful.
It's the thankful people who are happy."*

Unknown

Sheryl was a wildly successful woman. She came from humble beginnings but graduated at the top of her class in high school. She was accepted into Harvard, quickly emerged as a leader, and was their top economics student at the time. She received an MBA and eventually went on to work for the World Bank, as well as the U.S. Department of Treasury. Sheryl, now a billionaire, is the COO of Facebook.

However, in 2015, she experienced a tragedy that knocked her off her feet. One day while on vacation, Sheryl's beloved husband, Dave, went missing. She discovered him face down in the hotel gym. A healthy man in his forties with two young children, Dave passed away alone and unexpectedly.

Sheryl was devastated. No amount of money, educational prowess, success, or even well-meaning loved ones could console her during this time of loss.

Sheryl's story reminds us that this world can no doubt be a depressing and scary place. Greed and hate give way to war. Sickness and pain give way to death. Even in the absence of malady, all good things come to an end…and then we feel the loss.

How do we survive such a cold, harsh world? How did Sheryl move forward after her tragic loss? In her book, Option B, she gave us her answer: gratitude. We celebrate the good. We search for it and hold it closely. We create it. Gratitude helps us survive.

Although it's not easy, we've all practiced gratitude. Sometimes, it's as simple as stopping to literally "smell the roses." It may be sitting and reminisce with aging parents or laughing until your belly hurts with a group of friends. Practicing gratitude is one of the secrets to a happy life. In today's journal, write about how you practice gratitude for your blessings, as well as the things for which you are grateful.

I am grateful for: My parents

I will practice gratitude for this by: Visiting my parents weekly

I am grateful for:

I will practice gratitude for this by:

I am grateful for:

I will practice gratitude for this by:

I am grateful for:

I will practice gratitude for this by:

I am grateful for:

I will practice gratitude for this by:

I am grateful for:

I will practice gratitude for this by:

I am grateful for:

I will practice gratitude for this by:

I am grateful for:

I will practice gratitude for this by:

I am grateful for:

I will practice gratitude for this by:

$\mathcal{S}$ET APART

"A rose can never be a sunflower, and a sunflower can never be a rose. All flowers are beautiful in their own way."

Miranda Kerr

At our core, we are all the same. We all bleed red. We all have cells that make tissues, that make organs, that make…US! In this way, we are all the same.

Yet and still, we are all different. Very, VERY different. How paradoxical life is. We all possess the same basic makeup, yet our features manifest so differently…thank God! We are similar enough that no subset of people can truthfully claim to be biologically superior to another, yet diverse enough that we don't become lost in a sea of sameness. Understanding, acknowledging, and walking in this dichotomy is one path to personal fulfillment as we become who we truly are, rather than the carbon copies that the world tries to tell us we should be.

In today's journal, explore what sets you apart. How you are unique? How can you celebrate the diversity you bring to the world? How can you walk in and maximize that which makes you unique?

S ELF-MASTERY

"Mastering others is strength.
Mastering yourself is true power."

Lao Tzu

One might argue that all pain in the world stems from mankind's lack of self-control. Uncontrolled anger leads to bruised bodies and wounded souls. Uncontrolled greed leads to immense excess for some, yet lack and abject poverty for others. Historically, power left uncontrolled, has led to destruction and war.

Without question, mankind needs self-control.

Mastering the self is a lifetime task. Our desires must be tamed to meet the will of our true and highest selves. We must come to terms with knowing that, at the time, self-actualization may also mean self-denial. Whenever we exhibit self-control, we say to ourselves, "The person you are becoming is valuable to me. I will sacrifice to get you there." It's a decision that requires strength and discipline.

Write about a time that you showed restraint or self-control. What prompted you to do so? What does that experience tell you about yourself?

PATIENCE IS A VIRTUE

"Patience is not simply the ability to wait—it's how we behave while we're waiting."

Joyce Meyer

Remember what it was like to take a road trip when you were a child? Every twenty minutes, someone would ask the driver, "Are we there yet?" The monotony was only broken by periodic naps, snacks, and simple, deviceless games like "I spy." It seemed that it might take an eternity to reach the destination.

While road-trips may be a bit more tolerable now, patiently waiting for what we want as adults can still present a challenge. It requires that we slow down and resist the urge to rush forward, plowing over circumstances and people that delay our progress. We must hold our tongues, tame our emotions, and "check" ourselves. Those who master patience learn to savor the present, despite its deficiencies, problems, and quirks. Patience is indeed a virtue.

While perfect patience is an ever-moving target that we often miss, most of us have exhibited patience at various points in our lives. Perhaps it was while caring for a sick parent or loved one. Maybe it was while working on an arduous project. It might have even been while facing a belligerent driver with terrible road rage. Whenever it was, it need not be ignored

Record a time that you recall remaining patient in the face of a challenge. In what ways were you challenged? How do you feel about yourself having exhibited patience at that time?

WHEN NO ONE IS LOOKING

"Real integrity is doing the right thing, knowing that nobody's going to know whether you did it or not."

Oprah Winfrey

It's not difficult to do the right thing when we know we will be judged for it. We get to work on time when we know we have to clock in. We floss when we know we're going to the dentist. We even take extra care to clean up when we have company.

But what happens when we're given a job that implements the honors system for arrival and departure? Do we floss throughout the year? Do we take special care when we're the only ones that will see how we live? Who are we when no one is looking? In these moments, it becomes a little more difficult to do what's best.

Social approval is wonderful, but it has nothing on *self-approval*. When we operate with integrity, we can walk with heads high, knowing that we are showing up authentically and compassionately. We take the time to empathize and consider how our actions impact others. We have no reason to hide in shame because what we do in private is the same as what we do in public.

In today's journal, write about a time that you displayed integrity. How does it feel to explore this aspect of your character?

HE STAR THROWER

"I am only one, but I am one.
I cannot do everything, but I can do something.
And because I cannot do everything,
I will not refuse to do the something that I can do."

Edward Everett Hale

In a world filled with such tremendous need, it's easy to feel like your small contributions may not matter. Whether it's offering cash or a snack to a homeless veteran, caring for abandoned animals, or cleaning up local parks, we can take time to assist as best we can, but we can never seem to give enough.

While the need is great, small contributions still matter. One finger alone may not seem very threatening, but combine those fingers into a fist, and you can strike a mighty blow! Never underestimate the impact of your efforts to make this world better. The need may still exist, but your efforts matter to those you touch.

Loren Eiseley explains this phenomenon beautifully in his essay, "The Star Thrower." A little boy goes along the beach throwing starfish back into the sea after they had washed up on shore following a violent storm. There were tens of thousands of starfish to save and there was no way that the boy could save them all. However, when challenged by an older gentlemen who questioned how he could possibly make a difference, the boy reached down picked up another star, threw it into the ocean and said "It made a difference to that one."

You may not have ended world hunger, but perhaps you've fed one family. That matters! There a many stray animals with no homes, but did your puppy come from a shelter? That matters!

In today's journal, reflect on your own moments as "The Star Thrower." What are the charitable causes you have contributed time, resources, or talents over your life? What can you discover about yourself as you consider these contributions?

LESSONS LEARNED

"I never lose. Either I win, or I learn."

Nelson Mandela

The great thinkers in this world will tell you that we never truly lose in life; we either win, or we learn. Defeat can teach you to strategize. Heartbreak can teach you to choose wisely. And loss can teach you gratitude. Life is the greatest classroom one will ever enter.

The difference between winning and learning or winning and losing is simple: reflection. Learning requires us to go back and examine the situation and our decisions to look for cracks and holes that we may have missed. That knowledge is then stored in the backpack of our life experiences and can be pulled out for future reference. On the contrary, we lose when we view our failures as standalone experiences, unconnected to the greater picture of our lives, and unable to inform us of anything. We lose when we view every failure as final and unredeemable.

If you're human, you've undoubtedly experienced failure. While you may not have felt it at the time, your failures have made you a wiser person. You can walk more confidently into your next challenge, geared with data from your last failure; you just need to take some time to reflect on it.

In this journal, take some time to reflect on some of your past failures. Describe your role and what you might do differently in the future. What have you learned? Be careful not to berate yourself while discussing your role. You did the best you could with the knowledge that you had. Now you know better and are better because of it!

THE BEST GIFT EVER

"A wise lover values not so much the gift of the lover as the love of the giver."

Thomas à Kempis

Who doesn't like to receive a well-thought-out gift? It conveys care, consideration, and value to the recipient. It can strengthen healthy relationships and spark reconnection with long lost friends. A sincere and thoughtful gift can even pave the way to forgiveness and healing. These gifts need not have a large monetary value to be impactful. They simply need to speak directly to the hearts of the individuals for which they are intended.

While it's wonderful to be the recipient of a beautiful gift, it's even better to be the giver. Whether it be unexpected, long-awaited, or just because, when we bestow our feelings upon our loved ones in the form of a tangible gift, we are filled with joy and gratitude. It's an honor to be a conduit, stirring up happiness and excitement to the ones who mean most to us.

Providing just the right gift for just the right person can remind us of our own power and abilities. It shows that we can pay attention to understand and appreciate those around us. It proves that we have the power to change the world as we bring happiness to another human being.

Write about the best gift you have ever given. To whom was the gift given? How did that person respond? What can you learn about yourself from that experience?

# A BRAVE MOMENT

"Challenges make you discover things about yourself that you never really knew."

Cicely Tyson

There are times in life in which bravery goes unnoticed. We press forward, not because we are without fear, but because we know it is the only way to progress. Consider childbirth, for example. A woman goes into labor, afraid of the pain and uncertainty of the birthing process, yet she (literally) pushes forward.

These times of bravery in the face of fear and uncertainty show us our own strength and power. We learn that we can move forward, even when our emotions tell us otherwise.

It may seem like the opportunity to be brave only happens once in a lifetime or is reserved for soldiers and warriors, but truthfully, we are all brave more often than we realize. Maybe we give, not knowing where our own provisions will come from. Perhaps we stand up for someone without a voice, knowing that we may suffer as a result. Or maybe we simply wake up, get out of bed, and press forward, knowing that life is bringing more challenges with each rising sun. That's bravery.

When was the last time you showed bravery? What did you learn in the process? How did it feel to reflect on your own fortitude?

THE POWER IN A CHOICE

**"I am what I am today because of the choices
I made yesterday,"**

Stephen R. Covey

Life is a series of choices. Sometimes we choose well; other times, we miss the mark. It's so easy to dwell on the mistakes because we tend to feel the weight of those decisions much more severely. It goes back to that negativity bias. However, even when the poor choices set us back in major ways, they do not have to negate the positive choices. Those moments in life in which we "get it right" teach us how to trust ourselves. They show us that we do have the capacity to guide our own lives. They bring us blessings and opportunities. It's important not to ignore them.

What are some of the great choices you have made? How have they positively impacted your life? What can you learn about yourself as a result of this choice?

$\mathcal{S}$TANDING PROUD

"I am not a difficult woman at all. I am simply a strong woman and know my worth."

Unknown

There is often a misconception, particularly when it comes to women. It says that being proud is synonymous with being "cocky." While men are allowed to exude confidence, strength, and even arrogance, there's an unspoken rule applying only to women, which states that should we walk with confidence, unashamedly proud of our strengths, then we're also threatening, disingenuous, arrogant, or just really a terrible person. Many women have difficulty accepting compliments without berating some aspect of themselves, where a simple "Thank you" will do just fine. Although, as a whole, women are becoming bolder and less inhibited by patriarchal ideals, the idea of complimenting oneself is still foreign to many women.

The truth is that one can be proud, confident, and completely accepting of oneself, without acting as if others are less than. By definition, pride is simply the deep pleasure, gratification, or satisfaction we experience from our own achievements. The most enduring pride is pride in oneself, and the person that one is becoming.

Do you take pride in the person that you are? If so, what exactly are you proud of, and how can you continue to develop or celebrate this aspect of yourself? If you are not proud of who you are, what prohibits you? What is your plan to address this challenge?

THE DREAM TEAM

"Find a group of people who challenge and inspire you; spend a lot of time with them, and it will change your life."

Amy Poehler

Some people come into our lives and change us for the better. They show us our own strength and inspire us toward growth. They bring out our very best. These individuals help us smile on cloudy days and show us compassion when we feel that we deserve criticism. They are gifts from God.

We must be sure to convey our appreciation to these individuals. Without them, life would indeed be harder and much less sweet.

Write about the individuals who have contributed to your life in positive ways and brought out the best you have to offer. How have they impacted you? What can you learn about yourself from them? Most importantly, how can you appreciate and deepen your ties with them?

*J*UST SAY "NO"

"You can be a good person with a kind heart and still say no."

Lori Deschene

"Saying YES to happiness means learning to say NO to things and people that stress you out."

Time and chance happen to us all. This is a passage from the Bible that has been interpreted to mean that unexpected things, for which we can not prepare, will happen to everyone. No matter how health-conscious we become, we can fall terminally ill. We can be frugal and financially savvy, yet still experience debilitating financial blows. We can love deeply and attempt to be the perfect spouses, yet still experience heartbreak. At times, life can be a never-ending series of curveballs.

With the often unpredictable nature of the beast we call life, being intentional about how to spend our time is crucial. We twist ourselves into pretzels adjusting to unforeseen emergencies, the needs of loved ones, and day to day responsibilities. If not careful, this constant contorting can leave us unrecognizable to even ourselves. So, we must remain mindful of how we desire to live and how we desire *NOT* to live to remain true to the highest version of ourselves. This requires being able to say one simple word: NO.

Saying "no" is a powerful act that may require confidence to carry through. One has to be confident enough in her own ability to withstand the discomfort of disappointing someone else. Sometimes, she has to be confident in her ability to withstand ridicule or isolation, as well as conflict. A woman who says "no" values her time and personal convictions.

To what do you want to begin saying "no" to remain true to yourself and live on your own terms? Are there any actions you must take now to start the process? For example, do you need to let the board know that you will be stepping down next year or cancel a gym membership for a class you were pressured to take? Include how you plan to deal with the disappointment of other people when you begin setting boundaries.

CHANGE TAKES TIME

"Flowers don't worry about how they're going to bloom. They just open up and turn toward the light."

Jim Carrey

Have you ever sat and watched a rose bush bloom? Probably not. Why not? Probably because it would be such a painstakingly boring process of examination, waiting for change to occur. It would be impossible to appreciate the change that is happening with each passing moment!

So often, we fail to see our own emotional and psychological growth. After all, we live with ourselves every day. It's far easier to fall into the trap of constant self-examination and critique, rather than allowing ourselves to evolve naturally. What we fail to realize in this perpetual self-assessment is that growth typically happens in tiny increments, over periods. Eventually, when we look back over time, we notice that what was once a tiny sapling has evolved into a beautiful oak tree.

Take a moment to chronicle your own growth journey that perhaps you've been standing too close to see. Step back and consider where you were five, ten, or maybe just one year ago. You will surely see positive change.

If you're unsure of where to start, here's a prompt to help you out: "I no longer need."

$\mathcal{A}$ MILLION DOLLAR SMILE

"Nothing you wear is more important than your smile."

Connie Stevens

Rarely do we give smiling the credit it deserves. A properly timed smile can spark lifetime love between two strangers. It's a silent way of saying, "I see and value you" from way across the room. It's the simplest form of acknowledging humanity and demonstrating compassion for another. A smile is the universal language of kindness and joy.

Rather than obsessing about how to lose that last 10 pounds or sport the latest in designer fashion, what would it be like to focus on smiling more often? Smiling is the simplest way to become more attractive. You need not build up endurance or spend hours at the gym, nor will you need to invest any money. Smiling can even change your biochemistry, helping to release feel-good endorphins that will make you feel more invigorated and alive.

If you want to smile more, you will need to know what brings you pleasure. Due patriarchy and oppression, many women are disconnected from what gives them pleasure and as a result, they smile less. From the people and activities that you enjoy, to the textures, foods and images you love, take a second to explore what makes you smile. Why do they effect you as they do? How can you incorporate more of these factors into your life?

BEST KEPT SECRETS

"The universe buries strange jewels deep within us all,
and then stands back to see if we can find them."
Elizabeth Gilbert

The average human brain contains approximately 100 billion neurons. These neurons process and transmit information, playing a major role in our consciousness.

Imagine that! 100 billion working parts contribute to our thoughts. Our thoughts influence our behaviors, which ultimately determine how we show up in the world. This means that there is virtually no limit to our ideas. Our methods of self-expression are without end!

Remember when you were a child and nearly anything was possible? You wanted to grow up and be a unicorn? No problem! Felt like wearing pants AND a skirt? Consider it done. Your brain was a constant source of inspiration, uninhibited by the world's limits. You were sure to express every wild thought, emotion, and idea that floated into your consciousness… even if it meant telling some unassuming, nice adult that you didn't like the ugly sweater they gave you for your 5th birthday. The nerve of those adults, buying 5-year-olds sweaters instead of toys!

As adults, we often lose a great deal of that expression. We become stagnant and timid, revealing only the parts of ourselves that feel safe or "commonplace." Nevertheless, there are jewels of greatness inside each of us. It's our job to go out and reveal these treasures.

In today's journal, write about some of the jewels deep within. What are the best kept secrets you wish people knew about you? What treasures are you hiding? Why are they remaining hidden?

MANIFESTO

"If I didn't define myself for myself, I would be crunched into other people's fantasies for me and eaten alive."

Audre Lorde

Remember your teen years? That awkward time in which you were too independent to be babied and watched over, yet too inexperienced to be released into the world. You didn't yet understand the changes in your body or the shifts in your own personality. You desired to be accepted by your peers and loved by friends. At some point, your personal convictions were likely tested. In exchange for acceptance and approval, some kid asked you to act in a way that went against the core of who you were. But who exactly were you? Did you even know yet? If not, you probably struggled with these situations.

In life, there is no greater knowledge than knowledge and understanding of oneself. Self-awareness, self-reflection, and self-determination are crucial stones in the pillar of success and personal fulfillment. In this world, we will be many things to many people: daughter, sister, mother, friend, employee, boss, spouse. The roles will require us to contort, challenge, and transform ourselves in service of the relationship. As an actor in a play, we can easily become lost in the roles we play on the stage of life.

We can defend ourselves from loss of self, by determining who we are, before the rest of the world tells us who they would like us to be. So often, we fall into roles as life happens, twisting ourselves into pretzels in service of the roles we fulfill. We fail to consider whether or not we are acting in alignment with our true selves.

In today's journal, take a step towards self-determination. Write your personal manifesto. How do you intend to show up in this world? What are the most important values and desires you will carry into your decisions? What do you stand for, and how do you intend to live your life?

WHO ARE YOU, REALLY?

"Knowing yourself is the beginning of all wisdom."

Aristotle

Now that you have completed this phase of your confidence journey, you are likely stronger, wiser, and more in tune with who you are, as well as the working parts that make you nothing short of a miracle. For this final journal entry, refer back to your first entry in this journal. Note how your self-concept has changed. After having embarked on this journey of self-discovery, how would you now describe yourself to a stranger? Have you changed? Has your outlook on yourself changed? Note how you feel about your new self-concept? Do it make you proud, excited, hopeful about the future? How will you utilize this knowledge as you strive towards living out your personal manifesto written in the previous entry?

ACKNOWLEDGMENTS

Mom and Dad, there is no project that I will ever create for which I won't be able to thank you—you've given me the foundation to walk in my purpose. I know that I am supported in all that I do. I will always be thankful for that.

To my big, little brother, Cruise, thank you for all the tech support over the years—because…you know…I just can't! You are still the best SEO guy I know.

I can't forget the sister friends who have supported me all throughout my professional journey. You show up to the events. You share the posts. You speak the kind words of encouragement. Even more importantly, you remind me to celebrate even the smallest of victories and to be patient with myself. I would be a mess without you ladies!

To Jason, my media go-to. You saw many of my gifts in front of the camera, well before I did. Thank you for every photo, video, referral, and word of encouragement.

To Deborah, my editor, and the rest of my publishing team, thank you for being patient with me as I navigated to make this journey a success. I clearly could not have done this without you!

Finally, to the Most High God. You know I pray for purpose regularly. Thank you for unveiling my purpose early on, as well as equipping me with the gifts and the dream team to get there. You are so faithful!

ABOUT THE AUTHOR

 Kaity Rodriguez, LCSW, is a psychotherapist, confidence educator, and empowerment speaker with a passion for educating and inspiring girls and women to live amazing lives. Her counseling practice, Serenity Wellness, and Therapy Services, is located in Montclair, New Jersey, and she specializes in treating individuals with anxiety and stress disorders, as well as self-esteem and self-confidence issues. Kaity is a former Miss New Jersey USA and the author of Welcome to the Couch: A beginner's guide to therapy. She has been featured on media outlets such as FOX News, News 12 N.J., and NBC. This is her second book.